INTERNET PASSWORD NOTEBOOK

"Keep Track Of Web Addresses Usernames Passwords In One Easy & Organized Logbook"

AF271448

THIS BOOK BELONGS TO

_____

_____

_____

SOFTWARE INFORMATION

Software: _____
Purchase Date: _____
License Key: _____
_____

Software: _____
Purchase Date: _____
License Key: _____
_____

Software: _____
Purchase Date: _____
License Key: _____
_____

Software: _____
Purchase Date: _____
License Key: _____
_____

Software: _____
Purchase Date: _____
License Key: _____
_____

COMPUTER INFORMATION

Computer #1: _____

Model: _____

Serial Number: _____

Purchase Date: _____

Warranty: _____

Support: _____

Notes: _____

_____

Computer #2: _____

Model: _____

Serial Number: _____

Purchase Date: _____

Warranty: _____

Support: _____

Notes: _____

_____

Computer #3: _____

Model: _____

Serial Number: _____

Purchase Date: _____

Warranty: _____

Support: _____

Notes: _____

_____

NETWORK INFORMATION #1

ISP Name: _____

Website: _____

Account Number: _____

Email: _____

Password: _____

Support: _____

Notes: _____

_____

Modem/Router: _____

Model: _____

Serial Number: _____

Admin URL: _____

Username: _____

Password: _____

Notes: _____

_____

SSID (WiFi Network Name): _____

Password: _____

Security Mode: _____

Notes: _____

_____

NETWORK INFORMATION #2

ISP Name: _____

Website: _____

Account Number: _____

Email: _____

Password: _____

Support: _____

Notes: _____

_____

Modem/Router: _____

Model: _____

Serial Number: _____

Admin URL: _____

Username: _____

Password: _____

Notes: _____

_____

SSID (WiFi Network Name): _____

Password: _____

Security Mode: _____

Notes: _____

_____

A

Website: _____

Email: _____

Username: _____

Date/Password: _____

Date/Password: _____

Date/Password: _____

Notes: _____

_____

Website: _____

Email: _____

Username: _____

Date/Password: _____

Date/Password: _____

Date/Password: _____

Notes: _____

_____

Website: _____

Email: _____

Username: _____

Date/Password: _____

Date/Password: _____

Date/Password: _____

Notes: _____

_____

Website: _____

Email: _____

Username: _____

Date/Password: _____

Date/Password: _____

Date/Password: _____

Notes: _____

_____

Website: _____

Email: _____

Username: _____

Date/Password: _____

Date/Password: _____

Date/Password: _____

Notes: _____

_____

Website: _____

Email: _____

Username: _____

Date/Password: _____

Date/Password: _____

Date/Password: _____

Notes: _____

_____

A

Website: _____

Email: _____

Username: _____

Date/Password: _____

Date/Password: _____

Date/Password: _____

Notes: _____

_____

Website: _____

Email: _____

Username: _____

Date/Password: _____

Date/Password: _____

Date/Password: _____

Notes: _____

_____

Website: _____

Email: _____

Username: _____

Date/Password: _____

Date/Password: _____

Date/Password: _____

Notes: _____

_____

Website: _____

Email: _____

Username: _____

Date/Password: _____

Date/Password: _____

Date/Password: _____

Notes: _____

_____

Website: _____

Email: _____

Username: _____

Date/Password: _____

Date/Password: _____

Date/Password: _____

Notes: _____

_____

Website: _____

Email: _____

Username: _____

Date/Password: _____

Date/Password: _____

Date/Password: _____

Notes: _____

_____

B

Website:_____

Email:_____

Username:_____

Date/Password:_____

Date/Password:_____

Date/Password:_____

Notes:_____

_____

Website:_____

Email:_____

Username:_____

Date/Password:_____

Date/Password:_____

Date/Password:_____

Notes:_____

_____

Website:_____

Email:_____

Username:_____

Date/Password:_____

Date/Password:_____

Date/Password:_____

Notes:_____

_____

Website:

Email:

Username:

Date/Password:

Date/Password:

Date/Password:

Notes:

Website:

Email:

Username:

Date/Password:

Date/Password:

Date/Password:

Notes:

Website:

Email:

Username:

Date/Password:

Date/Password:

Date/Password:

Notes:

B

Website:

Email:

Username:

Date/Password:

Date/Password:

Date/Password:

Notes:

Website:

Email:

Username:

Date/Password:

Date/Password:

Date/Password:

Notes:

Website:

Email:

Username:

Date/Password:

Date/Password:

Date/Password:

Notes:

Website:

Email:

Username:

Date/Password:

Date/Password:

Date/Password:

Notes:

Website:

Email:

Username:

Date/Password:

Date/Password:

Date/Password:

Notes:

Website:

Email:

Username:

Date/Password:

Date/Password:

Date/Password:

Notes:

Website:—————————————

Email:—————————————

Username:—————————————

Date/Password:—————————————

Date/Password:—————————————

Date/Password:—————————————

Notes:—————————————

—————————————

Website:—————————————

Email:—————————————

Username:—————————————

Date/Password:—————————————

Date/Password:—————————————

Date/Password:—————————————

Notes:—————————————

—————————————

Website:—————————————

Email:—————————————

Username:—————————————

Date/Password:—————————————

Date/Password:—————————————

Date/Password:—————————————

Notes:—————————————

—————————————

Website: _____

Email: _____

Username: _____

C

Date/Password: _____

Date/Password: _____

Date/Password: _____

Notes: _____

_____

Website: _____

Email: _____

Username: _____

Date/Password: _____

Date/Password: _____

Date/Password: _____

Notes: _____

_____

Website: _____

Email: _____

Username: _____

Date/Password: _____

Date/Password: _____

Date/Password: _____

Notes: _____

_____

Website: _____

Email: _____

Username: _____

Date/Password: _____

Date/Password: _____

Date/Password: _____

Notes: _____

_____

Website: _____

Email: _____

Username: _____

Date/Password: _____

Date/Password: _____

Date/Password: _____

Notes: _____

_____

Website: _____

Email: _____

Username: _____

Date/Password: _____

Date/Password: _____

Date/Password: _____

Notes: _____

_____

Website: _____

Email: _____

Username: _____

C

Date/Password: _____

Date/Password: _____

Date/Password: _____

Notes: _____

_____

Website: _____

Email: _____

Username: _____

Date/Password: _____

Date/Password: _____

Date/Password: _____

Notes: _____

_____

Website: _____

Email: _____

Username: _____

Date/Password: _____

Date/Password: _____

Date/Password: _____

Notes: _____

_____

D

Website: _____

Email: _____

Username: _____

Date/Password: _____

Date/Password: _____

Date/Password: _____

Notes: _____

_____

Website: _____

Email: _____

Username: _____

Date/Password: _____

Date/Password: _____

Date/Password: _____

Notes: _____

_____

Website: _____

Email: _____

Username: _____

Date/Password: _____

Date/Password: _____

Date/Password: _____

Notes: _____

_____

Website: _____

Email: _____

Username: _____

Date/Password: _____

Date/Password: _____

Date/Password: _____

Notes: _____

_____

Website: _____

Email: _____

Username: _____

Date/Password: _____

Date/Password: _____

Date/Password: _____

Notes: _____

_____

Website: _____

Email: _____

Username: _____

Date/Password: _____

Date/Password: _____

Date/Password: _____

Notes: _____

_____

D

Website: _____

Email: _____

Username: _____

Date/Password: _____

Date/Password: _____

Date/Password: _____

Notes: _____

_____

Website: _____

Email: _____

Username: _____

Date/Password: _____

Date/Password: _____

Date/Password: _____

Notes: _____

_____

Website: _____

Email: _____

Username: _____

Date/Password: _____

Date/Password: _____

Date/Password: _____

Notes: _____

_____

Website: _____

Email: _____

Username: _____

Date/Password: _____

Date/Password: _____

Date/Password: _____

Notes: _____

_____

D

Website: _____

Email: _____

Username: _____

Date/Password: _____

Date/Password: _____

Date/Password: _____

Notes: _____

_____

Website: _____

Email: _____

Username: _____

Date/Password: _____

Date/Password: _____

Date/Password: _____

Notes: _____

_____

E

Website:_____

Email:_____

Username:_____

Date/Password:_____

Date/Password:_____

Date/Password:_____

Notes:_____

_____

Website:_____

Email:_____

Username:_____

Date/Password:_____

Date/Password:_____

Date/Password:_____

Notes:_____

_____

Website:_____

Email:_____

Username:_____

Date/Password:_____

Date/Password:_____

Date/Password:_____

Notes:_____

_____

Website:

Email:

Username:

Date/Password:

Date/Password:

Date/Password:

Notes:

Website:

Email:

Username:

Date/Password:

Date/Password:

Date/Password:

Notes:

Website:

Email:

Username:

Date/Password:

Date/Password:

Date/Password:

Notes:

E

E

Website: _____

Email: _____

Username: _____

Date/Password: _____

Date/Password: _____

Date/Password: _____

Notes: _____

_____

Website: _____

Email: _____

Username: _____

Date/Password: _____

Date/Password: _____

Date/Password: _____

Notes: _____

_____

Website: _____

Email: _____

Username: _____

Date/Password: _____

Date/Password: _____

Date/Password: _____

Notes: _____

_____

Website: _____

Email: _____

Username: _____

Date/Password: _____

Date/Password: _____

Date/Password: _____

Notes: _____

_____

Website: _____

Email: _____

Username: _____

Date/Password: _____

Date/Password: _____

Date/Password: _____

Notes: _____

_____

Website: _____

Email: _____

Username: _____

Date/Password: _____

Date/Password: _____

Date/Password: _____

Notes: _____

_____

E

Website:_____

Email:_____

Username:_____

Date/Password:_____

Date/Password:_____

Date/Password:_____

Notes:_____

_____

Website:_____

Email:_____

Username:_____

Date/Password:_____

Date/Password:_____

Date/Password:_____

Notes:_____

_____

Website:_____

Email:_____

Username:_____

Date/Password:_____

Date/Password:_____

Date/Password:_____

Notes:_____

_____

Website: _____

Email: _____

Username: _____

Date/Password: _____

Date/Password: _____

Date/Password: _____

F

Notes: _____

_____

Website: _____

Email: _____

Username: _____

Date/Password: _____

Date/Password: _____

Date/Password: _____

Notes: _____

_____

Website: _____

Email: _____

Username: _____

Date/Password: _____

Date/Password: _____

Date/Password: _____

Notes: _____

_____

F

Website: _____
Email: _____
Username: _____
Date/Password: _____
Date/Password: _____
Date/Password: _____
Notes: _____
_____

Website: _____
Email: _____
Username: _____
Date/Password: _____
Date/Password: _____
Date/Password: _____
Notes: _____
_____

Website: _____
Email: _____
Username: _____
Date/Password: _____
Date/Password: _____
Date/Password: _____
Notes: _____
_____

Website:_____

Email:_____

Username:_____

Date/Password:_____

Date/Password:_____

Date/Password:_____

Notes:_____

_____

F

Website:_____

Email:_____

Username:_____

Date/Password:_____

Date/Password:_____

Date/Password:_____

Notes:_____

_____

Website:_____

Email:_____

Username:_____

Date/Password:_____

Date/Password:_____

Date/Password:_____

Notes:_____

_____

G

Website: _____

Email: _____

Username: _____

Date/Password: _____

Date/Password: _____

Date/Password: _____

Notes: _____

_____

Website: _____

Email: _____

Username: _____

Date/Password: _____

Date/Password: _____

Date/Password: _____

Notes: _____

_____

Website: _____

Email: _____

Username: _____

Date/Password: _____

Date/Password: _____

Date/Password: _____

Notes: _____

_____

Website:_____

Email:_____

Username:_____

Date/Password:_____

Date/Password:_____

Date/Password:_____

Notes:_____ **G**

_____

Website:_____

Email:_____

Username:_____

Date/Password:_____

Date/Password:_____

Date/Password:_____

Notes:_____

_____

Website:_____

Email:_____

Username:_____

Date/Password:_____

Date/Password:_____

Date/Password:_____

Notes:_____

_____

G

Website: _____

Email: _____

Username: _____

Date/Password: _____

Date/Password: _____

Date/Password: _____

Notes: _____

_____

Website: _____

Email: _____

Username: _____

Date/Password: _____

Date/Password: _____

Date/Password: _____

Notes: _____

_____

Website: _____

Email: _____

Username: _____

Date/Password: _____

Date/Password: _____

Date/Password: _____

Notes: _____

_____

Website:

Email:

Username:

Date/Password:

Date/Password:

Date/Password:

Notes:

G

Website:

Email:

Username:

Date/Password:

Date/Password:

Date/Password:

Notes:

Website:

Email:

Username:

Date/Password:

Date/Password:

Date/Password:

Notes:

Website:

Email:

Username:

Date/Password:

Date/Password:

Date/Password:

Notes:

Website:

Email:

Username:

Date/Password:

Date/Password:

Date/Password:

Notes:

Website:

Email:

Username:

Date/Password:

Date/Password:

Date/Password:

Notes:

Website: _____

Email: _____

Username: _____

Date/Password: _____

Date/Password: _____

Date/Password: _____

Notes: _____

_____

H

Website: _____

Email: _____

Username: _____

Date/Password: _____

Date/Password: _____

Date/Password: _____

Notes: _____

_____

Website: _____

Email: _____

Username: _____

Date/Password: _____

Date/Password: _____

Date/Password: _____

Notes: _____

_____

Website:

Email:

Username:

Date/Password:

Date/Password:

Date/Password:

Notes:

Website:

Email:

Username:

Date/Password:

Date/Password:

Date/Password:

Notes:

Website:

Email:

Username:

Date/Password:

Date/Password:

Date/Password:

Notes:

Website: _____

Email: _____

Username: _____

Date/Password: _____

Date/Password: _____

Date/Password: _____

Notes: _____

_____

H

Website: _____

Email: _____

Username: _____

Date/Password: _____

Date/Password: _____

Date/Password: _____

Notes: _____

_____

Website: _____

Email: _____

Username: _____

Date/Password: _____

Date/Password: _____

Date/Password: _____

Notes: _____

_____

Website:_____

Email:_____

Username:_____

Date/Password:_____

Date/Password:_____

Date/Password:_____

Notes:_____

_____

Website:_____

Email:_____

Username:_____

Date/Password:_____

Date/Password:_____

Date/Password:_____

Notes:_____

_____

Website:_____

Email:_____

Username:_____

Date/Password:_____

Date/Password:_____

Date/Password:_____

Notes:_____

_____

Website:

Email:

Username:

Date/Password:

Date/Password:

Date/Password:

Notes:

Website:

Email:

Username:

Date/Password:

Date/Password:

Date/Password:

Notes:

Website:

Email:

Username:

Date/Password:

Date/Password:

Date/Password:

Notes:

I

Website: _____

Email: _____

Username: _____

Date/Password: _____

Date/Password: _____

Date/Password: _____

Notes: _____

_____

Website: _____

Email: _____

Username: _____

Date/Password: _____

Date/Password: _____

Date/Password: _____

Notes: _____

_____

Website: _____

Email: _____

Username: _____

Date/Password: _____

Date/Password: _____

Date/Password: _____

Notes: _____

_____

Website:_____

Email:_____

Username:_____

Date/Password:_____

Date/Password:_____

Date/Password:_____

Notes:_____

_____

Website:_____

Email:_____

Username:_____

Date/Password:_____

Date/Password:_____

Date/Password:_____

Notes:_____

_____

Website:_____

Email:_____

Username:_____

Date/Password:_____

Date/Password:_____

Date/Password:_____

Notes:_____

_____

Website: _____

Email: _____

Username: _____

Date/Password: _____

Date/Password: _____

Date/Password: _____

Notes: _____

_____

J

Website: _____

Email: _____

Username: _____

Date/Password: _____

Date/Password: _____

Date/Password: _____

Notes: _____

_____

Website: _____

Email: _____

Username: _____

Date/Password: _____

Date/Password: _____

Date/Password: _____

Notes: _____

_____

Website: _____

Email: _____

Username: _____

Date/Password: _____

Date/Password: _____

Date/Password: _____

Notes: _____

_____

Website: _____ **J**

Email: _____

Username: _____

Date/Password: _____

Date/Password: _____

Date/Password: _____

Notes: _____

_____

Website: _____

Email: _____

Username: _____

Date/Password: _____

Date/Password: _____

Date/Password: _____

Notes: _____

_____

Website:_____

Email:_____

Username:_____

Date/Password:_____

Date/Password:_____

Date/Password:_____

Notes:_____

_____

J

Website:_____

Email:_____

Username:_____

Date/Password:_____

Date/Password:_____

Date/Password:_____

Notes:_____

_____

Website:_____

Email:_____

Username:_____

Date/Password:_____

Date/Password:_____

Date/Password:_____

Notes:_____

_____

Website: _____

Email: _____

Username: _____

Date/Password: _____

Date/Password: _____

Date/Password: _____

Notes: _____

_____

Website: _____ **J**

Email: _____

Username: _____

Date/Password: _____

Date/Password: _____

Date/Password: _____

Notes: _____

_____

Website: _____

Email: _____

Username: _____

Date/Password: _____

Date/Password: _____

Date/Password: _____

Notes: _____

_____

Website:

Email:

Username:

Date/Password:

Date/Password:

Date/Password:

Notes:

K

Website:

Email:

Username:

Date/Password:

Date/Password:

Date/Password:

Notes:

Website:

Email:

Username:

Date/Password:

Date/Password:

Date/Password:

Notes:

Website:_____

Email:_____

Username:_____

Date/Password:_____

Date/Password:_____

Date/Password:_____

Notes:_____

_____

Website:_____

Email:_____

Username:_____

Date/Password:_____

Date/Password:_____

Date/Password:_____

Notes:_____

_____

Website:_____

Email:_____

Username:_____

Date/Password:_____

Date/Password:_____

Date/Password:_____

Notes:_____

_____

K

Website: _____

Email: _____

Username: _____

Date/Password: _____

Date/Password: _____

Date/Password: _____

Notes: _____

_____

Website: _____

Email: _____

Username: _____

Date/Password: _____

Date/Password: _____

Date/Password: _____

Notes: _____

_____

Website: _____

Email: _____

Username: _____

Date/Password: _____

Date/Password: _____

Date/Password: _____

Notes: _____

_____

Website: _____

Email: _____

Username: _____

Date/Password: _____

Date/Password: _____

Date/Password: _____

Notes: _____

_____

Website: _____

Email: _____

K

Username: _____

Date/Password: _____

Date/Password: _____

Date/Password: _____

Notes: _____

_____

Website: _____

Email: _____

Username: _____

Date/Password: _____

Date/Password: _____

Date/Password: _____

Notes: _____

_____

Website:_____

Email:_____

Username:_____

Date/Password:_____

Date/Password:_____

Date/Password:_____

Notes:_____

_____

Website:_____

Email:_____

Username:_____

Date/Password:_____

Date/Password:_____

Date/Password:_____

Notes:_____

_____

Website:_____

Email:_____

Username:_____

Date/Password:_____

Date/Password:_____

Date/Password:_____

Notes:_____

_____

Website:_____

Email:_____

Username:_____

Date/Password:_____

Date/Password:_____

Date/Password:_____

Notes:_____

_____

Website:_____

Email:_____

Username:_____

Date/Password:_____

Date/Password:_____

Date/Password:_____

Notes:_____

_____

Website:_____

Email:_____

Username:_____

Date/Password:_____

Date/Password:_____

Date/Password:_____

Notes:_____

_____

Website:—————————————————————

Email:——————————————————————

Username:—————————————————————

Date/Password:————————————————————

Date/Password:————————————————————

Date/Password:————————————————————

Notes:——————————————————————

————————————————————————

Website:—————————————————————

Email:——————————————————————

Username:—————————————————————

Date/Password:————————————————————

Date/Password:————————————————————

Date/Password:————————————————————

Notes:——————————————————————

————————————————————————

Website:—————————————————————

Email:——————————————————————

Username:—————————————————————

Date/Password:————————————————————

Date/Password:————————————————————

Date/Password:————————————————————

Notes:——————————————————————

————————————————————————

A B C D E F G H I J K L M N O P Q R S T U V W X Y Z

Website: _____

Email: _____

Username: _____

Date/Password: _____

Date/Password: _____

Date/Password: _____

Notes: _____

_____

Website: _____

Email: _____

Username: _____

Date/Password: _____

Date/Password: _____

Date/Password: _____

Notes: _____

_____

L

Website: _____

Email: _____

Username: _____

Date/Password: _____

Date/Password: _____

Date/Password: _____

Notes: _____

_____

Website:
Email:
Username:
Date/Password:
Date/Password:
Date/Password:
Notes:

Website:
Email:
Username:
Date/Password:
Date/Password:
Date/Password:
Notes:

Website:
Email:
Username:
Date/Password:
Date/Password:
Date/Password:
Notes:

M

Website: _____

Email: _____

Username: _____

Date/Password: _____

Date/Password: _____

Date/Password: _____

Notes: _____

_____

Website: _____

Email: _____

Username: _____

Date/Password: _____

Date/Password: _____

Date/Password: _____

Notes: _____

_____

M

Website: _____

Email: _____

Username: _____

Date/Password: _____

Date/Password: _____

Date/Password: _____

Notes: _____

_____

Website:

Email:

Username:

Date/Password:

Date/Password:

Date/Password:

Notes:

M

Website:

Email:

Username:

Date/Password:

Date/Password:

Date/Password:

Notes:

Website:

Email:

Username:

Date/Password:

Date/Password:

Date/Password:

Notes:

Website: _____

Email: _____

Username: _____

Date/Password: _____

Date/Password: _____

Date/Password: _____

Notes: _____

_____

Website: _____

Email: _____

Username: _____

Date/Password: _____

Date/Password: _____

Date/Password: _____

Notes: _____

_____

M

Website: _____

Email: _____

Username: _____

Date/Password: _____

Date/Password: _____

Date/Password: _____

Notes: _____

_____

N

Website:

Email:

Username:

Date/Password:

Date/Password:

Date/Password:

Notes:

Website:

Email:

Username:

Date/Password:

Date/Password:

Date/Password:

Notes:

Website:

Email:

Username:

Date/Password:

Date/Password:

Date/Password:

Notes:

Website: _____

Email: _____

Username: _____

Date/Password: _____

Date/Password: _____

Date/Password: _____

Notes: _____

_____

Website: _____

Email: _____

Username: _____

Date/Password: _____

Date/Password: _____

Date/Password: _____

Notes: _____

_____

Website: _____

Email: _____

Username: _____

Date/Password: _____

Date/Password: _____

Date/Password: _____

Notes: _____

_____

Website: _____

Email: _____

Username: _____

Date/Password: _____

Date/Password: _____

Date/Password: _____

Notes: _____

_____

Website: _____

Email: _____

Username: _____

Date/Password: _____

Date/Password: _____

Date/Password: _____

Notes: _____

_____

Website: _____

Email: _____

Username: _____

Date/Password: _____

Date/Password: _____

Date/Password: _____

Notes: _____

_____

Website: _____

Email: _____

Username: _____

Date/Password: _____

Date/Password: _____

Date/Password: _____

Notes: _____

_____

Website: _____

Email: _____

Username: _____

Date/Password: _____

Date/Password: _____

Date/Password: _____

Notes: _____

_____

Website: _____

Email: _____

Username: _____

Date/Password: _____

Date/Password: _____

Date/Password: _____

Notes: _____

_____

Website:

Email:

Username:

Date/Password:

Date/Password:

Date/Password:

Notes:

Website:

Email:

Username:

Date/Password:

Date/Password:

Date/Password:

Notes:

Website:

Email:

Username:

Date/Password:

Date/Password:

Date/Password:

Notes:

Website: _____

Email: _____

Username: _____

Date/Password: _____

Date/Password: _____

Date/Password: _____

Notes: _____

_____

Website: _____

Email: _____

Username: _____

Date/Password: _____

Date/Password: _____

Date/Password: _____

Notes: _____

_____

Website: _____

Email: _____

Username: _____

Date/Password: _____

Date/Password: _____

Date/Password: _____

Notes: _____

_____

O

Website:_____

Email:_____

Username:_____

Date/Password:_____

Date/Password:_____

Date/Password:_____

Notes:_____

_____

Website:_____

Email:_____

Username:_____

Date/Password:_____

Date/Password:_____

Date/Password:_____

Notes:_____

_____

Website:_____

Email:_____

Username:_____

Date/Password:_____

Date/Password:_____

Date/Password:_____

Notes:_____

_____

Website: _____

Email: _____

Username: _____

Date/Password: _____

Date/Password: _____

Date/Password: _____

Notes: _____

_____

Website: _____

Email: _____

Username: _____

Date/Password: _____

Date/Password: _____

Date/Password: _____

Notes: _____

_____

Website: _____

Email: _____

Username: _____

Date/Password: _____

Date/Password: _____

Date/Password: _____

Notes: _____

_____

Website:_____

Email:_____

Username:_____

Date/Password:_____

Date/Password:_____

Date/Password:_____

Notes:_____

_____

Website:_____

Email:_____

Username:_____

Date/Password:_____

Date/Password:_____

Date/Password:_____

Notes:_____

_____

Website:_____

Email:_____

Username:_____

Date/Password:_____

Date/Password:_____

Date/Password:_____

Notes:_____

_____

Website:_____

Email:_____

Username:_____

Date/Password:_____

Date/Password:_____

Date/Password:_____

Notes:_____

_____

Website:_____

Email:_____

Username:_____

Date/Password:_____

Date/Password:_____

Date/Password:_____

Notes:_____

_____

Website:_____

Email:_____

Username:_____

Date/Password:_____

Date/Password:_____

Date/Password:_____

Notes:_____

_____

Website:_____

Email:_____

Username:_____

Date/Password:_____

Date/Password:_____

Date/Password:_____

Notes:_____

_____

Website:_____

Email:_____

Username:_____

Date/Password:_____

Date/Password:_____

Date/Password:_____

Notes:_____

_____

Website:_____

Email:_____

Username:_____

Date/Password:_____

Date/Password:_____

Date/Password:_____

Notes:_____

_____

Website:_____

Email:_____

Username:_____

Date/Password:_____

Date/Password:_____

Date/Password:_____

Notes:_____

_____

Website:_____

Email:_____

Username:_____

Date/Password:_____

Date/Password:_____

Date/Password:_____

Notes:_____

_____

Website:_____

Email:_____

Username:_____

Date/Password:_____

Date/Password:_____

Date/Password:_____

Notes:_____

_____

Website:_____

Email:_____

Username:_____

Date/Password:_____

Date/Password:_____

Date/Password:_____

Notes:_____

_____

Website:_____

Email:_____

Username:_____

Date/Password:_____

Date/Password:_____

Date/Password:_____

Notes:_____

_____

Website:_____

Email:_____

Username:_____

Date/Password:_____

Date/Password:_____

Date/Password:_____

Notes:_____

_____

Website:_____

Email:_____

Username:_____

Date/Password:_____

Dale/Password:_____

Date/Password:_____

Notes:_____

_____

Website:_____

Email:_____

Username:_____

Date/Password:_____

Date/Password:_____

Date/Password:_____

Notes:_____

_____

Q

Website:_____

Email:_____

Username:_____

Date/Password:_____

Date/Password:_____

Date/Password:_____

Notes:_____

_____

Website: _____

Email: _____

Username: _____

Date/Password: _____

Date/Password: _____

Date/Password: _____

Notes: _____

_____

Website: _____

Email: _____

Username: _____

Date/Password: _____

Date/Password: _____

Date/Password: _____

Notes: _____

Q

_____

Website: _____

Email: _____

Username: _____

Date/Password: _____

Date/Password: _____

Date/Password: _____

Notes: _____

_____

Website:_____

Email:_____

Username:_____

Date/Password:_____

Date/Password:_____

Date/Password:_____

Notes:_____

_____

Website:_____

Email:_____

Username:_____

Date/Password:_____

Date/Password:_____

Date/Password:_____

Notes:_____

_____

Website:_____

Email:_____

Username:_____

Date/Password:_____

Date/Password:_____

Date/Password:_____

Notes:_____

_____

Website:

Email:

Username:

Date/Password:

Date/Password:

Date/Password:

Notes:

Website:

Email:

Username:

Date/Password:

Date/Password:

Date/Password:

Notes:

R

Website:

Email:

Username:

Date/Password:

Date/Password:

Date/Password:

Notes:

Website: _____

Email: _____

Username: _____

Date/Password: _____

Date/Password: _____

Date/Password: _____

Notes: _____

_____

Website: _____

Email: _____

Username: _____

Date/Password: _____

Date/Password: _____

Date/Password: _____

Notes: _____

_____

R

Website: _____

Email: _____

Username: _____

Date/Password: _____

Date/Password: _____

Date/Password: _____

Notes: _____

_____

Website:_____

Email:_____

Username:_____

Date/Password:_____

Date/Password:_____

Date/Password:_____

Notes:_____

_____

Website:_____

Email:_____

Username:_____

Date/Password:_____

Date/Password:_____

Date/Password:_____

Notes:_____

_____

Website:_____

Email:_____

Username:_____

Date/Password:_____

Date/Password:_____

Date/Password:_____

Notes:_____

_____

Website:_____

Email:_____

Username:_____

Date/Password:_____

Date/Password:_____

Date/Password:_____

Notes:_____

_____

Website:_____

Email:_____

Username:_____

Date/Password:_____

Date/Password:_____

Date/Password:_____

Notes:_____

_____

R

Website:_____

Email:_____

Username:_____

Date/Password:_____

Date/Password:_____

Date/Password:_____

Notes:_____

_____

Website: _____

Email: _____

Username: _____

Date/Password: _____

Date/Password: _____

Date/Password: _____

Notes: _____

_____

Website: _____

Email: _____

Username: _____

Date/Password: _____

Date/Password: _____

Date/Password: _____

Notes: _____

_____

S

Website: _____

Email: _____

Username: _____

Date/Password: _____

Date/Password: _____

Date/Password: _____

Notes: _____

_____

Website: _____

Email: _____

Username: _____

Date/Password: _____

Date/Password: _____

Date/Password: _____

Notes: _____

_____

Website: _____

Email: _____

Username: _____

Date/Password: _____

Date/Password: _____

Date/Password: _____

Notes: _____

_____

Website: _____ **S**

Email: _____

Username: _____

Date/Password: _____

Date/Password: _____

Date/Password: _____

Notes: _____

_____

Website: _____

Email: _____

Username: _____

Date/Password: _____

Date/Password: _____

Date/Password: _____

Notes: _____

_____

Website: _____

Email: _____

Username: _____

Date/Password: _____

Date/Password: _____

Date/Password: _____

Notes: _____

_____

S

Website: _____

Email: _____

Username: _____

Date/Password: _____

Date/Password: _____

Date/Password: _____

Notes: _____

_____

Website:_____

Email:_____

Username:_____

Date/Password:_____

Date/Password:_____

Date/Password:_____

Notes:_____

_____

Website:_____

Email:_____

Username:_____

Date/Password:_____

Date/Password:_____

Date/Password:_____

Notes:_____

_____

Website:_____ **S**

Email:_____

Username:_____

Date/Password:_____

Date/Password:_____

Date/Password:_____

Notes:_____

_____

T

Website:

Email:

Username:

Date/Password:

Date/Password:

Date/Password:

Notes:

Website:

Email:

Username:

Date/Password:

Date/Password:

Date/Password:

Notes:

Website:

Email:

Username:

Date/Password:

Date/Password:

Date/Password:

Notes:

Website: _____

Email: _____

Username: _____

Date/Password: _____

Date/Password: _____

Date/Password: _____

Notes: _____

_____

Website: _____

Email: _____

Username: _____

Date/Password: _____

Date/Password: _____

Date/Password: _____

Notes: _____

_____

Website: _____

Email: _____

Username: _____

Date/Password: _____

Date/Password: _____

Date/Password: _____

Notes: _____

_____

Website:_____

Email:_____

Username:_____

Date/Password:_____

Date/Password:_____

Date/Password:_____

Notes:_____

_____

Website:_____

Email:_____

Username:_____

Date/Password:_____

Date/Password:_____

Date/Password:_____

Notes:_____

_____

Website:_____

Email:_____

Username:_____

Date/Password:_____

Date/Password:_____

Date/Password:_____

Notes:_____

_____

Website:

Email:

Username:

Date/Password:

Date/Password:

Date/Password:

Notes:

Website:

Email:

Username:

Date/Password:

Date/Password:

Date/Password:

Notes:

Website:

Email:

Username:

Date/Password:

Date/Password:

Date/Password:

Notes:

T

Website:

Email:

Username:

Date/Password:

Date/Password:

Date/Password:

Notes:

Website:

Email:

Username:

Date/Password:

Date/Password:

Date/Password:

Notes:

Website:

Email:

Username:

Date/Password:

Date/Password:

Date/Password:

Notes:

Website: _____

Email: _____

Username: _____

Date/Password: _____

Date/Password: _____

Date/Password: _____

Notes: _____

_____

Website: _____

Email: _____

Username: _____

Date/Password: _____

Date/Password: _____

Date/Password: _____

Notes: _____

_____

Website: _____

Email: _____

Username: _____ **U**

Date/Password: _____

Date/Password: _____

Date/Password: _____

Notes: _____

_____

Website:

Email:

Username:

Date/Password:

Date/Password:

Date/Password:

Notes:

Website:

Email:

Username:

Date/Password:

Date/Password:

Date/Password:

Notes:

U

Website:

Email:

Username:

Date/Password:

Date/Password:

Date/Password:

Notes:

Website:_____

Email:_____

Username:_____

Date/Password:_____

Date/Password:_____

Date/Password:_____

Notes:_____

_____

Website:_____

Email:_____

Username:_____

Date/Password:_____

Date/Password:_____

Date/Password:_____

Notes:_____

_____

Website:_____

Email:_____

Username:_____

Date/Password:_____

Date/Password:_____

Date/Password:_____

Notes:_____

_____

Website: _____

Email: _____

Username: _____

Date/Password: _____

Date/Password: _____

Date/Password: _____

Notes: _____

_____

Website: _____

Email: _____

Username: _____

Date/Password: _____

Date/Password: _____

Date/Password: _____

Notes: _____

_____

Website: _____

Email: _____

Username: _____

Date/Password: _____

Date/Password: _____

Date/Password: _____

Notes: _____

_____

Website: _____

Email: _____

Username: _____

Date/Password: _____

Date/Password: _____

Date/Password: _____

Notes: _____

_____

Website: _____

Email: _____

Username: _____

Date/Password: _____

Date/Password: _____

Date/Password: _____

Notes: _____

_____

Website: _____

Email: _____

Username: _____

Date/Password: _____

Date/Password: _____

Date/Password: _____

Notes: _____

_____

V

Website:—————————————————————

Email:——————————————————————

Username:————————————————————

Date/Password:———————————————

Date/Password:———————————————

Date/Password:———————————————

Notes:———————————————————————

————————————————————————————

Website:—————————————————————

Email:——————————————————————

Username:————————————————————

Date/Password:———————————————

Date/Password:———————————————

Date/Password:———————————————

Notes:———————————————————————

————————————————————————————

Website:—————————————————————

Email:——————————————————————

Username:————————————————————

Date/Password:———————————————

Date/Password:———————————————

Date/Password:———————————————

Notes:———————————————————————

————————————————————————————

V

Website: _____

Email: _____

Username: _____

Date/Password: _____

Date/Password: _____

Date/Password: _____

Notes: _____

_____

Website: _____

Email: _____

Username: _____

Date/Password: _____

Date/Password: _____

Date/Password: _____

Notes: _____

_____

Website: _____

Email: _____

Username: _____

Date/Password: _____

Date/Password: _____

Date/Password: _____

Notes: _____

_____

Website:_____

Email:_____

Username:_____

Date/Password:_____

Date/Password:_____

Date/Password:_____

Notes:_____

_____

Website:_____

Email:_____

Username:_____

Date/Password:_____

Date/Password:_____

Date/Password:_____

Notes:_____

_____

Website:_____

Email:_____

Username:_____

Date/Password:_____

Date/Password:_____

Date/Password:_____

Notes:_____

_____

W

Website:_____

Email:_____

Username:_____

Date/Password:_____

Date/Password:_____

Date/Password:_____

Notes:_____

_____

Website:_____

Email:_____

Username:_____

Date/Password:_____

Date/Password:_____

Date/Password:_____

Notes:_____

_____

Website:_____

Email:_____

Username:_____

Date/Password:_____

Date/Password:_____

Date/Password:_____

Notes:_____

_____

Website:

Email:

Username:

Date/Password:

Date/Password:

Date/Password:

Notes:

Website:

Email:

Username:

Date/Password:

Date/Password:

Date/Password:

Notes:

W

Website:

Email:

Username:

Date/Password:

Date/Password:

Date/Password:

Notes:

Website:_____

Email:_____

Username:_____

Date/Password:_____

Date/Password:_____

Date/Password:_____

Notes:_____

_____

Website:_____

Email:_____

Username:_____

Date/Password:_____

Date/Password:_____

Date/Password:_____

Notes:_____

_____

Website:_____

Email:_____

Username:_____

Date/Password:_____

Date/Password:_____

Date/Password:_____

Notes:_____

_____

Website: _____

Email: _____

Username: _____

Date/Password: _____

Date/Password: _____

Date/Password: _____

Notes: _____

_____

Website: _____

Email: _____

Username: _____

Date/Password: _____

Date/Password: _____

Date/Password: _____

Notes: _____

_____

Website: _____

Email: _____

Username: _____

Date/Password: _____

Date/Password: _____

Date/Password: _____

Notes: _____

_____

X

Website:_____

Email:_____

Username:_____

Date/Password:_____

Date/Password:_____

Date/Password:_____

Notes:_____

_____

Website:_____

Email:_____

Username:_____

Date/Password:_____

Date/Password:_____

Date/Password:_____

Notes:_____

_____

Website:_____

Email:_____

Username:_____

Date/Password:_____

Date/Password:_____

Date/Password:_____

Notes:_____

_____

Website:_____

Email:_____

Username:_____

Date/Password:_____

Date/Password:_____

Date/Password:_____

Notes:_____

_____

Website:_____

Email:_____

Username:_____

Date/Password:_____

Date/Password:_____

Date/Password:_____

Notes:_____

_____

Website:_____

Email:_____

Username:_____

Date/Password:_____

Date/Password:_____

Date/Password:_____

Notes:_____

_____

Website:_____

Email:_____

Username:_____

Date/Password:_____

Date/Password:_____

Date/Password:_____

Notes:_____

_____

Website:_____

Email:_____

Username:_____

Date/Password:_____

Date/Password:_____

Date/Password:_____

Notes:_____

_____

Website:_____

Email:_____

Username:_____

Date/Password:_____

Date/Password:_____

Date/Password:_____

Notes:_____

_____

Website:

Email:

Username:

Date/Password:

Date/Password:

Date/Password:

Notes:

Website:

Email:

Username:

Date/Password:

Date/Password:

Date/Password:

Notes:

Website:

Email:

Username:

Date/Password:

Date/Password:

Date/Password:

Notes:

Website: _____

Email: _____

Username: _____

Date/Password: _____

Date/Password: _____

Date/Password: _____

Notes: _____

_____

Website: _____

Email: _____

Username: _____

Date/Password: _____

Date/Password: _____

Date/Password: _____

Notes: _____

_____

Website: _____

Email: _____

Username: _____

Date/Password: _____

Date/Password: _____

Date/Password: _____

Notes: _____ **Y**

_____

Website: _____

Email: _____

Username: _____

Date/Password: _____

Date/Password: _____

Date/Password: _____

Notes: _____

_____

Website: _____

Email: _____

Username: _____

Date/Password: _____

Date/Password: _____

Date/Password: _____

Notes: _____

_____

Website: _____

Email: _____

Username: _____

Date/Password: _____

Date/Password: _____

Date/Password: _____

Notes: _____

_____

Y

Website:_____

Email:_____

Username:_____

Date/Password:_____

Date/Password:_____

Date/Password:_____

Notes:_____

_____

Website:_____

Email:_____

Username:_____

Date/Password:_____

Date/Password:_____

Date/Password:_____

Notes:_____

_____

Website:_____

Email:_____

Username:_____

Date/Password:_____

Date/Password:_____

Date/Password:_____

Notes:_____

_____

Y

Website:_____

Email:_____

Username:_____

Date/Password:_____

Date/Password:_____

Date/Password:_____

Notes:_____

_____

Website:_____

Email:_____

Username:_____

Date/Password:_____

Date/Password:_____

Date/Password:_____

Notes:_____

_____

Website:_____

Email:_____

Username:_____

Date/Password:_____

Date/Password:_____

Date/Password:_____

Notes:_____

_____

Website:_____

Email:_____

Username:_____

Date/Password:_____

Date/Password:_____

Date/Password:_____

Notes:_____

_____

Website:_____

Email:_____

Username:_____

Date/Password:_____

Date/Password:_____

Date/Password:_____

Notes:_____

_____

Website:_____

Email:_____

Username:_____

Date/Password:_____

Date/Password:_____

Date/Password:_____

Notes:_____

_____

Z

Website: _____

Email: _____

Username: _____

Date/Password: _____

Date/Password: _____

Date/Password: _____

Notes: _____

_____

Website: _____

Email: _____

Username: _____

Date/Password: _____

Date/Password: _____

Date/Password: _____

Notes: _____

_____

Website: _____

Email: _____

Username: _____

Date/Password: _____

Date/Password: _____

Date/Password: _____

Notes: _____

_____

Z

Website: _____

Email: _____

Username: _____

Date/Password: _____

Date/Password: _____

Date/Password: _____

Notes: _____

_____

Website: _____

Email: _____

Username: _____

Date/Password: _____

Date/Password: _____

Date/Password: _____

Notes: _____

_____

Website: _____

Email: _____

Username: _____

Date/Password: _____

Date/Password: _____

Date/Password: _____

Notes: _____

_____

Z

NOTES

NOTES

Made in the USA
Monee, IL
07 July 2026

56551424R00066